W9-DGW-865

A Tale of Two Conversations:
Texting with Parents about Crushes **32**

❖ A Real Example: What's Wrong With This Convo? **34**

❋ Tip from a Bestie: How to Text Grown-Ups **36**

CHAPTER 3

Conversations in the Digital Age
Your Brain on Electronics:
What It Means to Be a Digital Native **38**

Texting, Social Media, and Interacting Online:
What's the Problem? **41**

Self-Esteem Online: You Are More than Your Likes **42**

Sharing the Knowledge **43**

But I Deleted It! Safety and Privacy Online **44**

PDOA (Public Display of Online Affection):
Relationships and Social Media **46**

Digital Vacations: Give Yourself a Break! **46**

❖ A Real Example: What's Wrong With This Convo? **48**

CHAPTER 4

Proceed with Caution
The Mighty Media Myths About
Stereotypes and Relationships **50**

Some Other Examples of Media Relationship Myths **52**

Opposites Attract...Sometimes! **55**

Where Will I Find My Next Friend or Crush? **61**

❖ A Real Example: What's Wrong With This Convo? **64**

CHAPTER 5

Leading a Balanced Life **66**

Developing a Crush on Your Life **69**

Don't Forget Your Friends **70**

❧ A Real Example: What's Wrong With This Convo? **74**

CHAPTER 6

The Nuts and Bolts of Communication
Starting a Conversation and Making Small Talk **76**

"Um...ah...you look nice."
(the Fine and Elusive Art of the Compliment **80**

Group Dates and Hang Outs **81**

Time Together/Time Apart **83**

Reading Body Language and Listening **83**

❧ A Real Example: What's Wrong With This Convo? **86**

❄ Tip from a Bestie: Screenshots Last Forever **88**

CHAPTER 7

Ouch! When Feelings Hurt **90**

Dealing with Jealousy **92**

Not Everyone Gets a Vote:
Dealing with Third Party Interference **94**

Age Differences in Relationships **95**

Fighting Fair: Boundaries and Consent **97**

Breaking Up Is Hard to Do (Sometimes!) **98**

HOW TO Text BOYS

♥♥♥♥♥♥♥♥♥♥♥

BY KELLI DUNHAM

APPLESAUCE PRESS

Kennebunkport, Maine

13-Digit ISBN: 9781604336320
10-Digit ISBN: 1604336323

This book may be ordered by mail from the publisher.
Please include $4.95 for postage and handling.
Please support your local bookseller first!

Books published by Applesauce Press Book Publishers are available at special discounts for bulk purchases in the United States by corporations, institutions, and other organizations.

For more information, please contact the publisher.

Applesauce Press Book Publishers
"Where good books are ready for press"
12 Spring St.
PO Box 454
Kennebunkport, Maine 04046
Visit us on the web at www.cidermillpress.com

Cover Design: Sara Corbett
Interior Design: Alicia Freile & Shelby Newsted
Typography: Fulham Road, Neutraface Slab Text,
Scala Sans LF, Pacifico, Rosewood, Helvetica

Printed in China
1 2 3 4 5 6 7 8 9 0
First Edition

Dedicated to Bryn Kelly who was— among many other wonderful qualities—an excellent texter of boys.

Table of Contents

INTRODUCTION

Why This Book?
What's Going on with My Friends?
What's Going on with My Life?! 8

❄ Tip from a Bestie: How to Text with Confidence 10

CHAPTER 1

Practice Makes Perfect
Developing Skills for Relationships
in Text and Face to Face 12

Does That Sound Overwhelming?
Don't Worry, We'll Take It One Step at a Time 13

This Book Is for Everyone 15

Stereotypes and Gender: In Text and Face to Face 15

❀ A Real Example: What's Wrong With This Convo? 18

CHAPTER 2

The Question of When
Am I Old Enough for a Crush? 20

How Do I Know If I'm Ready? 22

They Might Be Ready! I Know I'm Not! 26

Why Are Boys Such Kids Right Now!? 28

Talking with Parents:
What Are They so Worried about Anyway? 29

Stand Up for Yourself! **100**

Stand Up to Peer Pressure **102**

Stereotype Alert! The Double Standards in Dating **103**

Some Final Thoughts **103**

✤ A Real Example: What's Wrong With This Convo? **104**

✳ Tip from a Bestie: When to Put Down the Phone **106**

✳ ✳ ✳

Why This Book?

What's Going on with My Friends?
What's Going on with My Life?!

When you were younger, most of your social life was focused around your family and your parents. And it was usually the adults in your household who made decisions for you. But as you grow up, your friends and schoolmates become more important to you. You will get your first phone and make your first social media profiles—or maybe you already have! You will also start to make more decisions for yourself.

Sometimes it can be hard to know how to handle peer pressure, new friendships, crushes, and new responsibilities as you grow older, especially when more and more communication and social interaction moves online. But don't worry! We've got you covered. Whether you have questions about texting, social media, or the very first stages of dating—or even if you just wonder what all the fuss is about—this book is for you. This book is your guide to all the fuss.

TIP
from a
BESTIE

HOW TO TEXT WITH CONFIDENCE

"Friendships, crushes, parents, teachers—they're all complicated to deal with. "Smart phones" are supposed to make life easier, because it's right there in the name, right? It's a *smart* phone! But texting and social media actually make every relationship way trickier. As soon as my friends started getting their first iPhones in middle school, suddenly all of our convos were happening on our phones, even really important ones that should have been F2F. All of a sudden I felt like I needed to be texting everyone all the time because that's what everyone else was doing. I felt like I needed to learn a whole new language. And I also had to learn a whole new set of rules for how to text friends and crushes and grown-ups because everything was happening on my phone and not in person anymore. My biggest piece of advice for **how to text anyone**: if you wouldn't say it in person, don't send it in a text or Facebook message! And sometimes really important conversations need to be face-to-face, and there's nothing wrong with that!"

—Alex, *age* 15

CHAPTER 1

✳ ✳ ✳

Practice Makes Perfect

Developing Skills for Relationships in Text and Face to Face

I f the very idea of talking to someone makes you nervous, that doesn't mean this book isn't for you. It might not be right for you yet, or it might be a good time to learn all the important skills you will probably need later.

Learning dating and crush skills is like practicing your free throw during the summer before basketball season. Sooner or later, you'll have a chance to make that free throw and you'll be glad you spent the time practicing! So will your team...and your crush!

What kind of skills do you need to make a friendship or relationship work? Well, first you need to know what characteristics you're looking for in another person. It might seem like just picking the cutest person in your math class would be the best way to approach it, but the whole scene is a little more complicated than that. And once you've made some initial contact with your crush, you need to be able to communicate (that takes both talking and listening skills), learn about how to set and respect

boundaries, deal with conflict, and then (and this is especially important!) learn dating safety skills, for both online and in real-life encounters.

Does that Sound Overwhelming? Don't Worry, We'll Take It One Step at a Time

The good news is that every single skill you learn in your dating and crush quest, you can use in your daily life. Learning how to clearly ask for what you want is very important with a crush, but it's equally important when you're dealing with your parents. Setting boundaries is important with someone you're dating but it's also important with your friends.

Also, you might have noticed that as you are developing, you're getting some attention from those older than you who don't seem to understand that making certain kind of remarks to young girls and women is not okay. This is never your fault, but learning boundary setting and other relationship skills can give you more tools to deal with this unwanted and inappropriate attention.

Practice improves every time you try your hand at new skills, whether that's making real conversation with someone you have a crush on or hitting a curveball. At the same time, learning good habits is important to the success of all your future relationships and will make it easier to get a job or get into college or trade school and give back to your community.

This Book Is for Everyone

Throughout this book, you may have already noticed we say "crush" or "date" rather than "boyfriend." This is partly because we think "crush" and "date" better describe what it's like to "go out" with someone in your very early teen years. As we will talk about in the next chapter, labels like "boyfriend" can worry parents and adults, and they can carry a certain stigma, especially if you're not even sure about how hard you are crushing!

You should never feel guilty or awkward or even uncomfortable about any feelings of attraction that you may or may not have. If you're wondering about any of those thoughts or urges, we want you to know that this book is for you. And if you're not quite ready to think about dating yet, this book is for you, too. (You'll learn a lot about friendship as well!) The bottom line is that you should never hesitate to share what you're feeling with a trusted adult if you need some extra guidance!

Stereotypes and Gender: In Text and Face to Face

Some books written about dating make a really big deal about the differences between men and women, even going so far as to describe them as being from different planets. You'll notice we're doing things a little differently in this book.

Aside from some basic body differences (differences that become obvious during puberty), many of what we think of as differences between boys and girls are really only the result of social pressure to act or look a certain way. For example, there's no physical reason why girls should talk differently than boys.

But scientists who have studied language use have found that girls and women apologize much more in regular conversation and are less direct than boys and men are. This isn't because girls and women are actually so different from boys and men but because they are under social pressure to be so different. So while we'll talk about social influences and stereotypes, we're assuming that you and that boy in your math class are actually from the same planet.

▶ BOYS SAY...

Don't think we're confident just because we're acting cool. We're probably just as scared as you are about this whole dating thing, maybe even more! Sometimes when we tease you, we're not trying to be mean. We just can't figure out how to pay attention to you without being weird.

WHAT'S WRONG WITH THIS CONVO?

I n this chapter, we talk about developing the skills you need to enter the dating world and how there are sometimes social pressures to look and act a certain way that are not always okay. Usually, these situations are best addressed in person, not over text.

How would you have handled this situation differently if you were in Rosie's position? This would be a great opportunity to discuss this issue with the trusted adult in your life.

Rosie

Hey! That boy was weird again today.

What'd he do?

He said something weird about my skirt.

OMG that's not good! What'd u say?

Nothing. I didn't want him to stop the other boys from giving me a compliment.

Oh was the skirt thing a compliment???

I think he meant it to be.

OK but if you felt weird then it wasn't a compliment. Tell him to shut up next time.

Rosie (cont.)

That's so harsh tho.

What??? Stand up for yourself gurl.

***

CHAPTER 2

The Question of When

Am I Old Enough for a Crush?

The answer to the question "Am I old enough to date?" is: It depends. Which is probably the answer you get from the adults in your family who weigh in on this decision, right?

But it does depend. It depends on what you mean by dating. Phrases like "dating," "seeing someone," "going out," or even "going steady" can mean different things to different people. It's more important that everyone involved have the same definition of the terms.

For example, maybe your parents think "dating" means that you and your crush go out on dates to the movies and other places, spend time alone, are physically involved, and are planning a future together.

But maybe you think "dating" is when you text your crush a lot, or when your crush comes over and watches TV with you when your parents are home, maybe even in the same room.

Then let's say the first day of sixth grade you come home and announce: "I'm dating someone."

That might cause a very negative reaction. You might even see smoke come out of your parents' ears!

The question of whether you're "old enough" for crushes, romance, or dating is not actually about what grade you are in or how many candles you blew out on your last birthday cake. Being old enough to engage in dating and dating behavior is about having the skills and maturity to be safe and make good decisions.

It's a lot like riding a bike. You don't turn a certain age, wake up the next day, jump on your bike for the first time, and race down the biggest hill in your town. That would not be pretty!

Instead, you start small, with something that is easier to ride and has special safety features, like a bike with a big front wheel where you're only two inches from the ground. Then you graduate to a tricycle, and then a two-wheeler with training wheels. And then one day, after you've practiced a lot and built up strong legs and good balance, you take off the training wheels and you're riding all by yourself.

So, just like there are lots of different stages of learning to ride a bike, there are lots of stages to learning how to date and have romantic relationships. It works best if you take it slow, figure out what works and doesn't work in each stage, build up your skills, and then move on. If you jump in all at once...well, it won't look as bad on the outside as if you tried to ride your bike down the biggest hill, but it could mess up your feelings a lot!

How Do I Know If I'm Ready?

If you feel yourself starting to get interested in someone, to have romantic feelings, or even to have a crush, you might be

wondering if you are ready for some very low-key, limited-time, always-supervised dating.

The adults in your life will definitely have the last word on this, but it's important to think through these questions on your own:

❖ **Why am I interested in dating?** Do I have feelings of a crush or do I feel like I need to do this to be older and grown-up? Just because your friends are dating doesn't mean you should feel pressured. Friends, even close friends, might become interested in dating at different times. That's normal, even if it can be a little annoying to respond to your friend's 375,321 texts about her new crush. Although it can be difficult to resist peer pressure to date, especially if a friend wants you to complete a double date for a boyfriend's friend, it's better for everyone involved if you wait until you are really ready.

❖ **Am I able to set boundaries in a relationship and share that with another person?** A boundary is a guideline, an invisible line that keeps you safe in your dealings with other people. For example, if a friend does or says something that hurts your feelings, can you tell her you didn't like what she said, talk about it, and make it clear that it's not okay to say that thing to you?

❖ **Do I generally feel good about myself and my own abilities and characteristics?** If you feel good about yourself, it helps you make better choices about dating and crushes, and helps you set boundaries. If you are struggling with not feeling so great about yourself much or most of the time (everyone struggles some of the time), it might be better to work on that before introducing dating and crushes into the picture. You can talk to a trusted adult in your life about this; they might have some ideas on where to start.

❖ **If you've already had the first hints of those crush feelings, ask yourself, "Are my crushes on people who are likely to treat me well?"** We can't control who we are attracted to, but a lifetime of exposure to bad behavior presented as good behavior in the media (see the next chapter for more information) can sometimes make it harder to figure out the difference between the two.

❖ **Am I able to handle life's normal stresses and still concentrate in school, engage with friends, and take care**

of my responsibilities with my family? Dating can be awesome, but often there are ups and downs. If you have found ways to handle stress that work for you (talking it out, journaling, spending time in nature, exercising, etc.), you'll be more able to handle the extra emotional work that comes with being in a relationship.

✤ **Do I know how to self-soothe, that is, if my emotions are running high, do I know healthy ways to bring them back down to manageable levels?**

✤ **Do I have lots of other interests besides dating and crushes?**

✤ **Have I gotten the information I need about physical intimacy in dating (for example, kissing and beyond)? Do I understand the basics of how both girls' and boys' bodies work?**

And one more final and super important question:

✤ **Do I have a trusted adult who can answer my questions about dating, crushes, and this whole new area of my life?** Please note this trusted adult should not be named "the Internet." It's true there is a lot of information available online, but much of it is inaccurate and some of it is designed to scare young people into not dating or being physically involved.

The thing is, there is a lot in life to be legitimately afraid of: tigers, zombie movies, air conditioners falling out of windows. In dating, it's much better to be prepared rather than scared!

They Might Be Ready! I Know I'm Not!

If you don't feel any particular pull toward dating, or if you've looked at the list above and can say, "Whoa, that is definitely not me yet," maybe you aren't ready, and it's great and amazing that you know that.

NOPE

Just because you know that you aren't ready to date doesn't make it any easier to deal with the pressure around you. Here are some tips for handling it:

❖ Keep reminding yourself "there is nothing wrong with not being ready to date." If you are struggling with believing this, consult a trusted adult in your life who will probably be thrilled to support you.

❖ Spend less time with friends who are into dating, crushes, etc., and more with friends who have other interests.

Remember you don't have to get into any long explanation about why you are not dating. It's not anyone's business but your own. If people ask, you can say something general like:

✳ I'm not really interested right now.
✳ That's not where I am putting my energy at the moment.
✳ I've decided I'm not ready.
✳ I'm not up for that.

If you want, you can give a reason (for example, "I really have to work on my grades because I want to get into a special academic program this summer") but sometimes that's just like delivering an engraved invitation for your peers to argue with you. If all else fails, you can give your peers nonsensical answers like, "Oh, I'm actually an alien and I'm not allowed to date anyone on earth." Hopefully they will laugh and stop asking.

If someone close to you keeps bugging you about not dating, work on those boundary-setting skills: You can say, "Can you please stop asking? I am just not ready yet. How about I promise to let you know when I am ready?"

Emily

Hey do you think Charlie is cute?

Charlie? Why?

Uh because he's your lab partner. I see how you look at him.

He's fun, he's my friend.

But do you want to kiss him?

Srsly. I am not ready to date yet. I luv my single life.

OK but you better tell me when you kiss him.

OK but I am not dating him. Or anyone.

R U afraid?

Hey, really, please stop bugging me. U R my friend. I will tell you when I am ready.

Why Are Boys Such Kids Right Now!?

One difficulty of young teens and their crushes is that developmentally, boys take longer to get to the dating stage than girls. That doesn't mean that boys are immature; it just means that their puberty starts a little later, typically by about a year. You may have noticed a point in middle school when you and your friends had started thinking about crushes and dating, and the boys in your class were still making rude noises with their armpits. That was a perfect display of that year gap!

Again, this doesn't mean something is wrong with the boys, but if you are starting to get crush/dating feelings for those same boys and they respond with rude armpit noises, it can feel pretty weird for both sides. This is why girls this age often develop crushes on older boys. It isn't always bad to have a crush on a boy who is older than you by a year or so, but big age differences can sometimes lead to problems. More on that in Chapter 7.

Talking with Parents:
What Are They so Worried about Anyway?

Have your parents (and other adults in your life) started acting weird and awkward when they're talking about whether you're interested in dating, have crushes, etc.? It's true that sometimes even the most confident parents will be a little less confident talking about puberty, growing up, and dating.

You might give them a break. It's possible their parents never talked with them about these important subjects so they might want to chat with you but just don't know how.

Hint: If they gave you this book, they are trying to start a conversation. If you walk into the room holding this book in your hand and say, "I have a couple of questions..." you'll probably be able to get them to talk.

It's awesome if you can have this conversation even before you have a crush or are thinking about dating. Ask them about their hopes and fears for when you begin dating. Most parents have a lot of both. If you understand why they have set down guidelines, it might feel a little bit better than if all their rules seem random to you.

If your parents are very against you dating or being involved with crushes, it can be helpful to understand exactly what they're afraid of. Dating is scary to teens and it's scary for adults to watch their kids take their first steps into the adult world. Work on building trust and being open with them about your feelings. If they know they can at least trust you, you can build on that trust.

► MOMS SAY...

It might seem like we don't want you to be happy when we put restrictions on your dating life. But we know you are under lots of pressure to be grown up and to seem grown up, and we want you to have a chance to enjoy all the parts of your life and not to be rushed into the next stage by outside pressure.

And yeah okay, we're also worried about you dating. It's not that we don't trust you (unless you've given us a reason not to trust you), it's that we don't trust the outside world. We know that dating can hurt sometimes and that we can't protect you from everyone and everything.

And you know what else we're worried about? That we haven't prepared you. That we haven't given you the right information and talked enough about dating. Or maybe that we've talked too much! And we know you've been watching our relationships and dating choices closely, and we're hoping you won't make the same mistakes we've made, whether those mistakes were big ones or little things!

A Tale of Two Conversations:
Texting with Parents about Crushes

Let's say you want to talk with your parents about someone you have a crush on. You can never 100 percent predict what will make the conversation go well, but here's an example of two conversations; one will most likely go better than another.

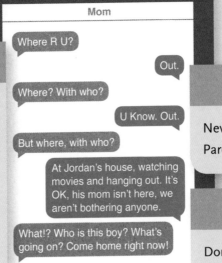

TIP

Scared parents are unhappy parents. Here, Mom is afraid that you are alone in the house with a boy you have a crush on. Even if you know nothing much will happen, it's the kind of thing parents worry about. And with good reason.

TIP

Never say "out." Parents hate "out."

TIP

Don't wait until you're in trouble to bring up the crush.

Versus this conversation, same situation:

Mom

I am at my friend Jordan's house. Can I stay until 8?

Who is Jordan?

A friend from school. Maybe I have a little crush on him. Not sure.

What?!

Sorry, I was embarrassed to tell you in person. I just want to get to know him better. We R watching videos and talking in the living room. His mom isn't home but his older brother is watching us.

Okay but be home by 8. NO LATER!!!

Thanks!

TIP

Yay! You texted before she was checking up on you.

TIP

Sometimes it's hard to talk to a parent about a crush. If it is, you can tell your parent that it's hard and that makes the whole thing less awkward. Parents were kids once too!

TIP

If you arrive home on time, your parents will be more likely to let you go out again!

WHAT'S WRONG WITH THIS CONVO?

I t's hard enough to know if you're ready to date or not. Sometimes, friends are ready before you are and can be very excited to share this new interest. It can be hard to navigate these new waters, and sometimes this causes a strain on your friendship. Here is an example of this disconnect between friends.

Show this conversation to your friends and make a plan for how to handle this situation if it ever comes up. Try setting a time (after homework is done!) when you can talk about crushes, or come up with a code for when one of you is distracting others.

TIP
from a
BESTIE

HOW TO TEXT GROWN-UPS

"

I never really thought about how much I'd text adults when I got my first iPhone—I kind of figured I'd just text my friends all the time. But grown-ups text almost as much as I do, so I had to learn real quick that texting adults is way different from texting my friends. I babysit on the weekends and parents text me to schedule jobs. I have to be super professional with them when I'm texting so they know I'll be responsible with their kids. My biggest piece of advice for **how to text adults:** use full sentences (not abbreviations and emojis) and be respectful. I use their last names, like: 'Hi Mrs. Whalen, do you still need me to babysit on Friday?' Even though *everyone texts everyone* no matter how old you are, there are definitely different rules to follow depending on who's getting the messages."

—Shelby, age 16

✳✳✳

CHAPTER 3

Conversations in the Digital Age

Your Brain on Electronics: What It Means to Be a Digital Native

If you are a girl born after 1980 (and chances are, if you are reading this book, you are), you are considered a "digital native." What this means is that under most circumstances, you can't remember a time before "being online" was a thing. In some ways, this means that your primary culture is the Internet, and that you expect to be constantly connected to anyone you want to be connected to, no matter where they are.

Exactly how connected you are varies a little, even within other girls your same age. For example, if your family can't afford or doesn't permit preteens to have smart phones, you might be slightly less connected than a friend who has been carrying a cell phone since the day she stepped out of diapers.

However, these small differences in connectedness are tiny when compared with the difference between how connected your

parents were with their friends and family, and how connected you are with yours.

For example, just a few decades ago, the average teenager didn't have private access to any phone, much less a phone that was just theirs. Instead, they might talk to their friends while standing in the middle of the family room, or in a hallway, trying to make the curly phone cord (yes, phones were connected to the wall) reach into a hall closet for privacy. And if their parents were waiting for an important call? No one would even be allowed to touch that phone!

Contrast this with an average preteen or teenager today who may have access to not only a smart phone of their own, but also a personal computer and numerous other ways to communicate: video calls, texts, photo texts, all sorts of social media apps, anonymous social media apps, 30-second videos that disappear after you watch them, etc.

This means that the way you interact with your friends is different, and this also means the way you approach dating is different. This chapter addresses some of the good and bad parts of being constantly connected and will hopefully guide you to make good decisions about how to make technology serve you, instead of your smart phone bossing you around!

Even though it might seem like non-digital natives (that is, the adults in your life) don't get the difficulty and complications of dating in today's world, you can be sure that many of the feelings are the same, even though the modes of communication are different.

The first time you reach out to a crush and tell them you like them, it is always a little scary and a lot awkward. You are going to feel like your stomach is doing backflips. That is part of growing up. It doesn't matter whether you are calling from a phone while standing in your parent's kitchen, or making the contact via instant message or text.

Texting, Social Media, and Interacting Online: What's the Problem?

The advantages of all this constant connection seem pretty obvious: If you want to talk to your friend, you talk to them. If you want to reach out to a crush, you can reach out to them. You don't have to wait to do it. You also don't have to worry about quickly trying to think of something clever, interesting, or funny to say in reaction to what they said. With text and most forms of instant messaging, you can think about what you say, exactly how it will be understood, and what it says about you before you hit send.

The things that make being constantly connected seem awesome sometimes make it not-so-great as well. Talking in real-life works different muscles than texting does; you have to be more spontaneous, and read someone's emotional state based on their body language. You also have to listen carefully to

someone's tone of voice to understand what they mean because there aren't any emoticons in real-life conversation!

Communicating online also makes it possible to multitask to an almost ridiculous point. How many times have you found yourself sending text messages on your phone while you watch a movie on your laptop, instant message on your favorite social media site, and send short video chats, all at the same time? All this multitasking might seem like a really good way to connect with lots of people, but the problem is that we aren't actually wired as human beings to connect in this way. We need more real-life interactions and conversations that go deeper than "What's up?" In fact, experts who study human interaction and technology have figured out that people who spend more time on social media are actually more lonely than people who interact with less people, but have their interactions in real-life.

Self-Esteem Online: You Are More than Your Likes

Why does spending a lot of time on social media make us lonely? One of the biggest reasons is we feel pressure to always present our best self. If you are having a terrible day, like you just failed a math test, have a cold, or are fighting with your best friend, your selfie probably won't show you looking miserable. You'll put on a cute duck face and smile.

When everyone else around you is posting about their great luck, how they're feeling good, love their new boyfriend, and did great on their math test, you might start wondering why you are such a failure. But you're comparing what you know about your inside feelings with everyone else's public self, presented in good light and on a good hair day.

Sharing the Knowledge

Because you read this book, you know all the ways that technology can be a challenge to friendships and relationships. Is there a way to share that without seeming like a know it all? How about:

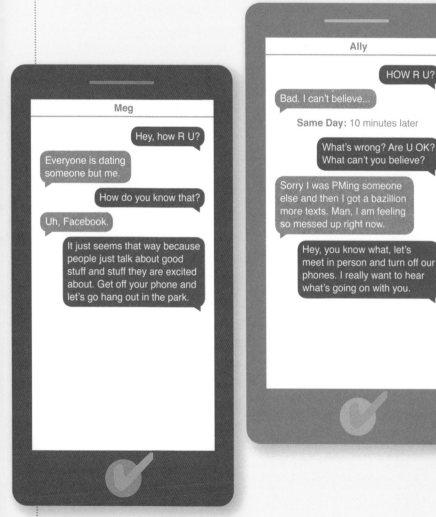

Meg

Hey, how R U?

Everyone is dating someone but me.

How do you know that?

Uh, Facebook.

It just seems that way because people just talk about good stuff and stuff they are excited about. Get off your phone and let's go hang out in the park.

Ally

HOW R U?

Bad. I can't believe...

Same Day: 10 minutes later

What's wrong? Are U OK? What can't you believe?

Sorry I was PMing someone else and then I got a bazillion more texts. Man, I am feeling so messed up right now.

Hey, you know what, let's meet in person and turn off our phones. I really want to hear what's going on with you.

But I Deleted It! Safety and Privacy Online

You have probably heard this before (maybe 100 times), but the number one thing you need to remember about the cyber world is that nothing you put out into the world electronically is ever really private.

For example, sometimes girls feel pressure from boys they are dating to send photos of themselves dressed a certain way or hardly dressed at all. Even young teens sometimes feel this pressure, especially if the person they are dating sends a photo like this first. You should *never* feel like you have to send any kind of photo of yourself to anyone who asks for it, whether it is someone you are dating, a crush, or even just a friend.

It might be best to say no. Ask yourself before you send any text, message, video, or photo out there: "Would it be okay with me if everyone in my whole world saw this post/text/photo? Not just the person I am sending it to, but my teachers, family, all my friends, strangers, my babysitter from when I was a little kid, and my grandma and grandpa?"

There are apps that let you post anonymously and apps that claim videos you send disappear after they are watched, but you know that doesn't really protect you because you know screenshots exist. Once it's out there, you aren't in control of your image anymore. You've created an electronic trail that is impossible to erase.

The trail doesn't have to be made on purpose to cause you problems. If you share a photo with your best friend who is very loyal and would never share it without your permission, she could still lose her phone at school and the photo could end up in someone's hands who might not be loyal to you. Or the

photo could be forwarded accidentally. Or it could be accidentally uploaded to an app.

It's important to remember that almost everyone you meet online is a stranger. And the adults in your life have definitely warned you about talking to strangers, right? If anyone you don't know in real-life contacts you online and wants to meet with you in real-life, let a parent or another trusted adult know.

It's also important to use common sense about how much information you share online about where you are. If you're going to use the "check in" feature in social media apps, make sure these posts are sent to friends (specifically people you know in real-life) only. Your whereabouts don't need to be accessible to everyone with a computer and online access.

PDOA: Public Display of Online Affection: Relationships and Social Media

If you have a crush or are going with or dating someone, it's important that both of you understand what is okay to post on social media and what is not okay. This will be different for each couple, but it needs to be an agreement you come to together.

Talk with your crush about whether it is okay to tag you in photos and check you into locations, and whether your relationship will be "social media official" or whether you'd rather keep it more private. You should also talk about whether it's okay to post, talk, or tweet about your relationship and whether you can use each other's devices. Even if you occasionally use a date's phone to send a quick email or message, it is not a good idea to share passcodes: everyone needs privacy and there is no reason for dates to be checking each other's texts!

Digital Vacations: Give Yourself a Break!

It may seem like with all this talk about responsibility, privacy, and safety concerns, adults in your life would be glad if electronic communications just—poof—disappeared and we all went back to just yelling when we wanted to talk with someone who isn't in the room.

No, electronic communication is here to stay and can be a positive force in your life—and in your social and dating life—if you learn to control it, instead of it controlling you.

Some ways to get control of your online and electronic connectivity are listed on the next page!

✤ Pick quality of interaction over quantity of interaction. Instead of belonging to every single social media site, pick one or two that work best for you, and limit friends to people you are actually friends with, not people that you have only met once or twice. Use social media to plan for activities in real-life, instead of letting it be a substitute for real-life activities.

✤ When you start to date someone or have a crush, try to have equal time interacting with them in real-life. There are lots of things you can't learn about someone by just texting, and real-life interactions are also fun!

✤ When possible, work on school or art projects with your friends and classmates in person, not just online.

✤ Experiment with participating in an activity (a sports event, concert, etc.) with friends or a crush or a date without taking photos, posting about it online, etc. You might find that it's a very different kind of experience!

✤ Take a day off from screens every once in awhile. You should be able to have an occasional personal day where you don't have to be instantly available to everyone you know. You might really like having the time to think, and you might even want to make it a habit!

Or maybe not. But it's worth a try. If nothing else, your social media free day will give you something new to post about on social media!

WHAT'S WRONG WITH THIS CONVO?

You now know after reading this chapter that not everything posted on the Internet is anonymous or safe. It's always important to keep in mind just who could read everything you post, even if you do so "anonymously": your teacher, the principal, your parents, and so on!

Bevin

Saw ur status. U R babysitting this Saturday?

Yeah, gotta watch my baby bro.

No parents?

Nope!

That's cool, but dude u gotta keep that stuff offline.

Why? It's just a status. No1 even liked it.

Yeah but everyone can see. Is your page private?

I dunno???

OMG dude u should really check that out.

Bevin (cont.)

It's not like I put up my address!

Anyone can creep online and figure it out. Please be careful.

Ur no fun! I just want everyone to know what's going on.

✳ ✳ ✳

CHAPTER 4

Proceed with Caution

The Mighty Media Myths about Stereotypes and Relationships

I f you have already started having crushes or what could be romantic feelings for someone, you might be surprised by how strong these feelings are. **You may have also discovered that these strong feelings can't be changed easily.** You can't usually wake up one morning and say "I'm not having this crush anymore" or "I think I should have a crush on..."

This is why it's important to think about what you are looking for in a crush and how you expect someone you're dating to treat you before you get involved.

One reason for this is that the media (and the world in general) is full of images of negative relationship behavior presented as positive relationship behavior. A simpler way of saying this is that we see lots of examples of people acting messed up when they're dating someone, but no one is calling it messed up!

How many times have you seen an example of something like this in a movie: The female star is talking about why she and the male star can't work out being together. The male star doesn't look

like he's listening, He grabs her and—even though she is trying to push him away—he kisses her. She struggles for a minute and then gives in and kisses back and—guess what—all of a sudden all their relationship problems are solved and now they can live happily ever after.

Kissing someone who doesn't want you to kiss them definitely does not solve relationship problems. It's not romantic. It's actually gross and unethical because you're violating the other person's consent! (Much, much more coming on consent in Chapter 7.)

When we see this kind of thing too much, it can make it hard to judge what is and isn't okay in relationships.

Some Other Examples of Media Relationship Myths

✤ **Myth:** Jealousy in a relationship shows how much the other person cares about you; the more jealous your date gets, the more they must like you!

✴ **Fact:** It is normal for people who are dating to have occasional jealous feelings or need to talk out a situation where one person feels jealous, but when someone is jealous most of the time or demands you behave in a specific way so they won't feel jealous, this usually means that they are insecure and are trying to manage their feelings by controlling you.

Hint: A little jealousy occasionally in a relationship is normal, but it's something to talk about and work through. It shouldn't be a constant thing.

❖ **Myth:** Relationships are a cure for being lonely. If you are lonely you need to be in a relationship.

❋ **Fact:** Everyone feels lonely sometimes, even people who have lots of friends or are in a relationship. If you rush into a dating situation with the idea it will be an "instant cure" for your loneliness, you might not make the best choice of a person to date. And being in a relationship with someone who is a bad choice for you can be even more lonely than being single!

Hint: If you're feeling lonely, it might help to put energy into making new friends who like the same activities as you do.

❖ **Myth:** If you're in a good relationship, the person will know what you want and need without being asked.

❋ **Fact:** Being crushed out on someone doesn't mean you can read their mind! Learning to ask for what we need is a very important skill for any relationship, not just romantic ones.

Hint: Even if it's hard to ask for what you need, you can still do it. You can even start your request by saying, "So this is really hard for me to ask but..." and then continue with your request.

❖ **Myth:** Once you find your one true love or soul mate, you will live happily ever after.

✳ **Fact:** Hopefully no one has convinced you that you will find your one true love in eighth grade! But even for adults, meeting someone they feel very connected to is just the beginning of the story. Every relationship, including really good ones, takes a lot of work.

Hint: The work probably shouldn't take more time than the fun stuff, especially at first.

❖ **Myth:** Being in a relationship proves you are mature. Or pretty. Or a "good catch."

✳ **Fact:** Being in a relationship doesn't prove that you are attractive, a good catch, or even mature. In fact, often teen and preteen girls who are more mature aren't too worried about dating because they are more interested in school, activities, and hobbies.

Hint: It's hard not to compare yourself to other girls your age, but everyone grows up in different ways at different times. Wherever you are in the process is probably good for you.

✤ **Myth:** No one can be happy when they are single.

✳ **Fact:** It's true that older people who are in committed happy relationships do tend to be healthier and live longer. We don't know for sure if the relationship actually causes the good health, or if people who are already healthy are more likely to be in relationships. However, for young people, especially those under thirteen, the exact opposite is true. Young people who are what experts call "early daters" have more difficulty with development into their teen years, take bigger risks, and show more signs of stress than young people who wait until later in their teens to date.

Hint: Waiting until YOU know you are ready to date will make you much happier than trying to go by someone else's timetable.

Opposites Attract...Sometimes!

Once you've got some of that media clutter out of your brain about what relationships should be, you can think more clearly about what kind of relationship you would like.

What kind of characteristics do you think are important in someone you might date? You probably already have some ideas, even if you're years away from having your first crush: they are the qualities you look for in friends!

Sometimes people develop crushes based on what someone looks like or the kind of clothes they wear or how popular they are. And we can't always control who we feel attracted to; sometimes we just get butterflies in our stomach when the person walks by. That can be fun, but if you're going beyond a crush on someone you might actually have a conversation with, you might not want to choose a potential date based on the fact that they wear a certain kind of shoes, have a tight haircut, or wear fancy bow ties, even if you find these things attractive. You might think about other characteristics that make it fun to spend time with a crush: honesty, sense of humor, generosity, maturity, and being able to talk about lots of different subjects.

Some characteristics you might be looking for include:

❖ Loyalty (a person who supports you in your daily life)

❖ Humor (someone who can laugh at themselves is a particular catch!)

❖ Intelligence

❖ Being fun (especially being chill enough to deal with things going a little wrong on a date)

❖ Good hygiene (showers are pretty important!)

❖ Good manners (how does the person talk to their parents? Other kids? Other adults?)

❖ Knows how to listen (really listen, not just waiting for their turn to talk)

❖ Open to trying new things

❖ Has outside interests (not just dating and not just video games)

❖ Independent (not always concerned with what other people think about them)

❖ Similar values to yours

❖ Sensitivity to your feelings (notices when you are upset, or can deal with you being upset)

In addition to the above qualities, there are other qualities known as temperament traits that might be part of what you are looking for in a date. Temperament traits are something you are born with and that usually don't change much, even when you're an adult. Different temperament traits are part of what determines how we react to different situations. Temperament traits are the way you are in the world and how you experience the world. It's easiest to think of them as being on a sliding scale; everyone falls somewhere along the continuum in every area of temperament.

For example, one temperament characteristic is mood. At one end of the continuum is optimism. An optimistic person usually thinks that things are going well, or will go well, and tends to see situations are more positive. On the other end of the mood continuum is pessimism; when a person is generally more serious and more likely to focus on negative things in a situation.

It's important to remember when we talk about temperament—especially temperament in relationships—that being on one side or another is not objectively good or bad. But if you and your date are not at similar places on the continuum, sometimes this can cause arguments or at least misunderstandings.

Let's talk about how that might look in real-life.

Matt and Molly are in all the same classes at school and have recently begun texting and decided they like each other. Both their parents are pretty strict, and they definitely aren't allowed to go on actual dates. However, after they have been saying they are "going together" for a few months, they do get permission to go to the park one day after school as part of a group, as long as they text their parents when they arrive and when they're leaving. The park day comes and it looks like the weather is about to go bad.

Matt and Molly text each other before school. Matt, who tends to be optimistic, says, "I am sure it will be okay, I have a good feeling about this." Molly, who is more pessimistic, responds "Sigh. It's going to rain for sure. Figures. SMH."

Matt is annoyed and wonders if Molly's response is because she doesn't really want to go to the park with him. Molly is annoyed and wonders if Matt's response is because he doesn't really care if they get to go to the park or not.

MATT & MOLLY

When they meet after school, it turns out the sun has come out, and they are able to make their park date as planned. Matt reminds Molly, "I told you it would be okay." Molly opens her bag and shows Matt her umbrella and says, "Yes, but I planned in case it wasn't okay!"

In this case, because of their temperament differences (optimistic versus pessimistic), Matt and Molly reacted differently to a situation and this led the other person to jump to conclusions or imagine something about what their date was thinking.

It's important to recognize that temperament differences don't always have to cause problems if you can understand the differences between yourself and someone else as just differences, not one person being wrong and one person being right. For example, Matt could appreciate that Molly planned for rain instead of just hoping for the best, and Molly could appreciate that Matt was cheerful because he didn't spend all day worrying about the rain.

Some other temperament traits:

❖ Persistence: How long a person stays with something they care about.

❖ Activity level: How much a person prefers to run around or be moving around.

❖ Intensity: How big a person's reaction is to situations. A very intense person might jump around when they are mad, a less intense person might just get quiet.

❖ Approach/withdrawal: How easy it is for the person to try new things or meet new people.

❖ Sensory sensitivity: How sensitive a person is to things that reach them through the five senses (sight, hearing, smell, taste, touch). Some people are very sensitive to things like light or sound, other people might like the lights up high and the music up really loud.

It's helpful if you think about where you fit in within these temperament traits and whether someone else being similar is important to you. For example, if you are a very intense person, it might be confusing or hard for you to hang out with someone who has a more mild reaction to situations. Or you might be able to hang out with someone who is less intense, and learn how to have slightly less intense reactions when things happen. This is all different for different people. It's just important to remember that there is no right or wrong when it comes to temperament: It's about being different or similar, and how that feels to the people involved in an interaction.

Sometimes our feelings about temperament might be influenced by stereotypes we have about gender. For example, because boys are often given the message that "real men don't cry," they may be less willing to be open about their sensitivity or intensity in certain ways. So a boy who is very intense might react with what looks like anger, even if he is feeling sadness. Something similar might be true for girls who are told it isn't ladylike to show anger; if you're a girl who tends toward intensity, you might feel pressure to cry instead of showing your anger in another way.

Just like you don't need to feel ashamed of being a girl who gets mad sometimes, you can make the world a better place by not giving a boy who expresses sadness a hard time. Feelings are not right or wrong—they just exist. Of course, you already know we do have to use care in how we express our strong feelings—especially anger—in order to treat others with respect. But remember that the emotions themselves are not good or bad, even if they don't match with how some people say a girl should feel.

Where Will I Find My Next Friend or Crush?

So, now you've studied the media myths about relationships, thought about characteristics you are looking for in a date, and figured out some of your own temperament characteristics and what characteristics are likely to be compatible with you. Congrats, you are so far ahead of many adults who are playing the dating game!

At this point, if you've read this far, there's probably a good chance you already have a crush on someone so this next section might not apply to you. But if you're thinking of dating and crushes in a more "maybe some day" kind of way, it's helpful to know there are good and not-so-good places to meet future crushes.

Here are some positives and negatives for crushing and dating in different parts of your life.

School

✳ **Positives:** Spend lots of time together, get to know their friends and see how they treat other people, their teachers, etc.

✿ **Negatives:** Might distract from studying (it's hard enough to learn algebra without your crush sitting between you and the board), might be awkward if you break up and have to look at them opening their locker every day.

Sports teams and other after-school activities

✳ **Positives:** Have time together without distractions during the school day.

✤ **Negatives:** Hard to compete with someone you have a crush on, schedules tend to change (for example, what happens at the end of the soccer season?).

Community organizations
(for example, Boy or Girl Scouts, church, service organization, etc.)

✳ **Positives:** More likely to have similar values, families may know each other.

✤ **Negatives:** Possibly less time together, organization may have rules about young people dating other young people in the program (be sure to check with an adult in-charge first).

You may have noticed that "the Internet" is not included on the list of possible places to meet crushes. I bet you can guess why: No adult would ever buy a young person a book that suggested that they should look for dates online. Ever. This is because there are huge safety concerns for young people meeting online, and there is no way to eliminate the risk completely. See the next chapter for more about how you can use technology to help build, rather than hurt, relationships.

WHAT'S WRONG WITH THIS CONVO?

The Mighty Media Myths strike again! One of the many things this chapter covered was traits to look for in a crush and how they might be influenced by gender stereotypes. Just like how girls are told they should be ladylike, the following text conversation shows another stereotype: boys are told not to cry.

How would you handle a conversation like this? What other things would you point out to Trina?

Trina

I don't like Lamar anymore.

Y?

Cuz when we watched that stupid movie about the Wreck of the Edmund Fitzgerald in social studies class, he cried!

So?

So he's a weirdo.

Wait. What?

He cried during the movie.

I don't get it.

OMG he cried. In class. With everyone.

So? I was crying too.

Trina (cont.)

OMG OMG OMG he was crying like a girl!

Whatever. I don't care if a boy cries. Lamar is just sensitive IMO.

U R weird.

CHAPTER 5

*** ❋ ***

Leading a Balanced Life

At times, it might seem like every girl your age has a boyfriend or a girlfriend, a date, a boo, or a crush. It also might seem like even girls who aren't dating are always talking about someone they have a crush on, or going back and forth about who likes whom.

If you're not interested or ready for all this talk, it can be a little overwhelming. **The important thing to remember is wherever you are on your quest for romantic relationships is normal for *you*.**

Not interested yet? That's just fine.

Not interested now? That's also just fine.

Interested but haven't felt any feelings for anyone special? This is also a perfectly okay place to be with your feelings.

Even though all these feelings are perfectly normal, when you're surrounded—or feel surrounded—by girls talking about crushes—you might start to feel sad or annoyed, or at least a little left out.

Some reassurance: It might feel like you are the only girl in the entire seventh grade who is single, but that probably isn't true. And even if every girl in your grade except you is dating someone

(Hey, where do you go, Romance Junior High?), you can encourage yourself with this important fact: Learning how to be single is an important life skill.

Although you'd never know it from Hollywood-created romantic comedies, most adults will spend time in their life as a single person. Some people even prefer single life! Being single in seventh grade might not always be a huge party, but it can be fun, and it can be (ugh, here it comes again) a great learning experience.

What are some advantages of not dating or having a crush?

❖ More energy for your friends and family. Remember those are relationships too, and just as important (and possibly longer lasting) than romantic ones!

❖ Your fingers don't get sore from texting constantly, and your neck might feel better from not constantly looking down at your phone.

❖ More time for schoolwork. Maybe that doesn't feel like an advantage. But if you're struggling with algebra, having a few extra minutes for tutoring or practicing problems can mean the difference between getting it and being lost!

❖ Easier to go away with your family, on vacation for example, if you're not always worried about what your crush is doing while you're gone.

❖ More time to get better at your favorite video game. Or your not-so-favorite video game. Or even take up a hobby that doesn't involve any kind of device that needs to be plugged in or charged!

Developing a Crush on Your *Life*

It sounds pretty corny, but NOT dating can be a great way to develop a crush on yourself and your own life. You can get to know yourself better by spending time alone or with friends who aren't worried about dating yet.

You can even spend some time daydreaming. While it's hard for girls who have always had a smart phone in their hand to imagine, experts believe your brain actually grows and recovers from all the stimuli it has experienced when you're just sitting there not doing anything in particular. Please don't use this as your excuse for not paying attention in math class though.

Those "not ready for dating" times are also opportunities for you to get involved in activities that help you develop skills for the future. Maybe you could build your leadership abilities by running for student council at school, or you can develop your compassion and caretaking abilities by volunteering at a nursing home. Learning a musical instrument can also be a great way to use your time and energy that you're not investing in crushes. Maybe you can even write "I've got a crush on my afterschool activities" love song with your new ukulele skills.

Or maybe not. But you get the idea.

Don't Forget Your Friends!

Once crushes come into the picture, it can be easy to put aside friendships for your crush. But it's important to make time for your friends, too. Friends hold your history: Who else is going to remember that time you got a black eye because you didn't catch

the can of soda they threw for you at the mall? Or when you lost a tooth during class in first grade?

Just remembering that friendships with your girl friends are special relationships can help keep them safe from being crushed by your crush, but of course you also need to spend time with your friends to reassure them this is true. Continue the traditions and rituals of friendships (meeting before school, texting on Saturday mornings) even when you have a crush. And talk about things other than your crush when you're together with your friends. Your friends can also give you important feedback about how spending time with your romantic interest is impacting your everyday life. They might even give you more feedback than you want!

HELP! I HAVE A CRUSH!

Part of having a crush is being tempted to turn the rest of your life upside down to spend time with the person you like. And let's face it, the overwhelming feeling that you absolutely MUST see, spend time with, or message with your crush can be part of what makes having a crush so exciting.

It can also make things feel out of control. But one sign of being mature enough to handle some early dating is to know how to slow down your time with your crush so that it doesn't take over your life.

❖ Have limits about when and how much you text or message. This is especially important on school nights when it's easy to get caught up in a fun and flirty exchange, and then realize, "Oh no, it's 3 a.m. and I have to get up at 6 a.m. for school!" Short of actually removing your phone or computer from where you sleep, the adults in your life can't really control this, so you will have to show self-control. It may not seem possible, but you actually can turn your phone off!

❖ Ask your crush to help you keep boundaries around your time together. You can say something like, "Tom (only if his name is Tom), I have been so tired the last couple of mornings because we've been up so late texting. Can we please make an agreement to stop at midnight when we have to be at school the next morning?"

✤ Keep a close eye on any regular activities that might be slipping because you're concentrating on your crush. If thinking about your date is keeping you from studying, packing the nutritious lunch you usually take to school, or going to soccer practice, maybe you need to sort out your priorities!

✤ Look for early warning signs of Crush Takeover in your life, and then take whatever steps you need in order to get the right balance again. Otherwise, the adults in your life might take those steps for you, and that probably won't be very fun for you...or your crush!

WHAT'S WRONG WITH THIS CONVO?

Don't forget your friends! Grab your friends and talk about how to handle this conversation. Is there a day that can be "Girls Only"?

Hope

When R we hanging out next?

I'm busy this weekend.

What about after school? 2nite?

I can't.

2morrow?

Um naw. sorry.

Should I just talk to ur secretary? Do you have a calendar where u keep your super busy schedule? U can put me in there like I'm a dentist appointment.

Huh?

U R always busy now

??

...

Hope (cont.)

Cuz you have a boyfriend.

U kno I have wanted a boyfriend 4 so long. Y can't U just be happy 4 me? I thought you were my friend. And U know how much I like Charlie. I can't believe this!

I didn't think you having a boyfriend would = me never seeing U.

U see me at school!

That's not the same. U know what I mean.

No I don't kno what you mean.

CHAPTER 6

***

The Nuts and Bolts of Communication

Starting a Conversation and Making Small Talk

I f you watch your older siblings making friends, talking with crushes, or asking people out, you might think, "How did they get so smooth? They've got game."

Or, depending on your older siblings, you might not think that at all.

But conversation skills, small talk—even smoothness—can all be learned. And while you have to practice to get better, the basic skills are pretty simple.

The beginnings of small talk (that somewhat random conversation people make in the beginning of a social interaction) pretty much follows a formula that looks like this:

Relevant statement + question = interaction.

An example might help here. Let's say you walk into Social Studies class early and there is your crush, sitting by himself, maybe fiddling with his phone, but not surrounded by friends like he usually is. This is your perfect time to talk to him, but how do you start?

Follow the small talk formula! First make a relevant statement. This is usually a comment on the physical environment, something you can see in the area, or a recent event.

For example you might say, "I can't believe how many chapters we had to read."

But don't stop there, that puts too much burden on the other person to create the conversation. Instead follow up with a related question.

For example, you might ask, "What did you think about that long story about the Louisiana Purchase?"

The statement gives context for your follow-up question so it doesn't seem so random, and the question itself invites the conversation to start. You could also make a statement about the weather, an app both you and your crush use, or a school activity you have in common.

Note that you don't want to ask closed questions, questions that can be answered with just a yes or a no; if you do that, the conversation can end pretty quickly. Also beware of giving one or two word replies yourself. Saying "I guess" or "uh-huh" doesn't move the conversation along.

Don't be afraid of awkwardness; feeling a little bit awkward is a part of developing the art of conversation. Even if you don't know what to say in response to what your crush says, just responding without completely changing the topic can be helpful and get the conversation over an awkward patch.

If starting conversations like this feels weird, practice with your friends. Being able to initiate talking with someone you don't know is a great social skill to have now and at any age. Since not everyone has the skill, the person you're trying to talk with will probably be relieved that you took the chance.

Six Great Questions to Keep a Conversation Going:

1 Have you ever taken a plane? A cross-country train or bus? Where were you going? Did anything interesting happen on that trip?

2 Who taught you about loyalty?

3 What can you do better than anyone else in your family?

4 What was it like the first time you stayed away from home overnight?

5 Do you remember your first day of kindergarten? What were you most scared of?

6 What is your favorite photo on your phone/on social media? Why is that photo so important to you?

"Um...ah...you look nice." (the Fine and Elusive Art of the Compliment)

Compliments can be a great way to start a conversation, if you can think of one that makes sense based on your interactions with your crush. Here are some compliments that are likely to be greeted warmly:

"Hey, I was really impressed with how you balanced that equation in chemistry lab last period."

"I like that hoodie a lot. Does it have a story?"

"Did you get your hair cut? It looks awesome."

Of course, making an extra effort to start a conversation in this way can feel like a risk. What if the other person doesn't respond in a positive way or doesn't respond at all? Learning to deal with rejection could make a book all its own, but it's important to remember that making the effort and taking the risk is the only accurate way to figure out how interested the other person might be in you. It can really hurt and feel awkward to be rejected, but you will have some small, personal satisfaction in knowing you gave it a try.

BOYS SAY...

We asked boys what they wished girls knew about how to communicate with them. Here's what they said:

 ✻ Don't be scared to make the first move or send the first text! Boys can be chicken, but it doesn't mean we don't like you.

 ✻ Don't get frustrated if a boy is slow in texting you back. We don't text that much and our thumbs don't work as fast!

 ✻ We love it when you learn something about what we love...like video games (for some of us, at least).

Group Dates and Hang Outs

If you have a crush or a potential date, and are looking to get to know a crush better, a group date is a great way to make that happen. Group dates can mean different things to different people, but mostly it's just a fun, collective gathering of friends. An important aspect of a group date that makes it actually work is having a real activity planned. Just hanging at someone's house isn't a great group date because there are no natural ways to interact with your crush beyond just talking.

A lot of times, everyone just ends up fooling with their phones, watching videos, or playing video games, which also doesn't really help you get to know someone else better.

So what are some group hang outs? They don't have to be expensive if you're creative about it. What is available will depend on where you live and how easily you can get around, but some ideas include:

❖ Going to a school sports activity or presentation

❖ Completing a group craft project

❖ Participating in a group service project, like serving food at a soup kitchen

❖ Heading to a bookstore to hear your favorite author read or talk about their books

Hint: You can often negotiate with parents for a group date when they won't even consider you and your crush hanging out together alone.

Time Together/Time Apart

No matter what you call your new crush/date/person, when you first are getting to know each other, it's easy to want to spend every moment together. This is natural and normal, but it also has some drawbacks, like making it hard to concentrate on your schoolwork, extracurricular activities, or stay in touch with your other friends.

If you can, arrange to take breaks from each other every now and then, for example: "We don't text on weeknights between 4:30 p.m. and 6:00 p.m. so we can concentrate on homework" and "every Saturday morning, I get together with my buddies for softball and that is friends-only time."

Giving each other a little room in this way not only shows a lot of maturity, it also keeps adults in your life from coming up with their own plans to make sure you do your schoolwork!

Reading Body Language and Listening

Getting to know someone else isn't just about learning to talk—it's also important to listen to the other person: both the words they say and the nonverbal cues they send out while they're talking.

When you are having a conversation, it's important to demonstrate that you're listening and not just waiting for the other person to stop talking. Sometimes this means waiting a few moments when the other person stops speaking before you start to talk. This can be especially hard if you're nervous because we always want to fill every moment of silence.

When you listen, make eye contact with the person who is talking. You don't have to stare at them or look at them every single moment (that might seem creepy), but make sure it's clear they have your attention and you aren't, for example, looking down at your phone.

An important part of listening is asking prompting questions, for example, "Really, wow, what happened next?" or "So what did you say then?" Try to avoid generic responses like "Uh huh" which make you sound bored and not present. Developing good listening skills is a short cut to social success. If you are a good listener, everyone around you will think you are brilliant without you saying a word!

It's helpful to both read other people's body language and to be aware of what your own body language is showing. Fidgeting and looking away or looking at your phone shows your crush/friend/teacher that you're not really interested in what they have to say. Crossed arms send the same message.

If you lean toward the other person a little when they're speaking (not too much; it shouldn't feel like you are about to fall over) and smile when appropriate, you'll make them feel listened to and valued.

Seven Ways to Be a Great Date/Crush/ Partner (and pssst, Even a Great Friend!):

1 Listen.

2 Listen even when your date is talking about something that bores you.

3 Remember important days and important people in your date's life. Ask about these days and people, for example, "Oh your grandma was going to have cataract surgery right? How is she doing?"

4 Pay sincere compliments. Tell them you like or admire something they have done or the way they handled a situation. The more specific, the better. "You're um...nice" isn't much of a compliment at all.

5 Remember little things about their preferences and try to make those happen for them. If your crush loves ginger ale, make sure there is always a can in the refrigerator when they come to visit.

6 Remember the things they don't like, too, and offer to help make those things easier. For example, offer to bring them a sandwich when they're studying for a hard test.

7 Ask the question "Is there anything you need right now?" and listen to your crush's response.

WHAT'S WRONG WITH THIS CONVO?

Communication can be tough, especially when your body can be saying something different! We covered body language and listening, both of which are at odds in this text conversation!

How should Phil and his girlfriend solve this? What would you have said instead? This may be a great way to talk about body language with your crush or friend, too!

TIP
from a
BESTIE

SCREENSHOTS LAST FOREVER

"Texts don't seem super permanent, right? It's like, I send a million texts a day, and my phone deletes them after like thirty days, so it's no big deal. Except that one time, someone took a screenshot of something kind of mean that I said, and then they texted the screenshot to the girl I said it about. I felt so bad—it really hurt her feelings. It really made me realize that even though texting feels private, your texts can become public before you know it. My biggest piece of advice for **how to text cautiously** is to remember that anyone can take a screenshot of anything, and those screenshots last forever."

—*Jasmin, age 13*

CHAPTER 7

* * *

Ouch!

When Feelings Hurt

Part of the difficulty of relationships, especially crushes, dates, and romantic relationships, is that **they can bring up very strong feelings.** In fact, if your parents or other adults responsible for you are worried about you dating too young, often what they are most worried about is you getting hurt and not yet having the skills and emotional resilience to recover from it.

Just like it's important to know how to start a conversation, give a compliment, and pay special attention to special people in your life, learning how to deal with conflict, difficulties, and break ups are important skills you need to enter the dating world.

This isn't a fun part, but it's really important. And the more skills you have and the better you understand negative relationship patterns, the easier it will be for you to get through the hard stuff.

Dealing with Jealousy

Almost everyone feels jealous at one time or another, and it doesn't take a crush or date to make us feel that way. We can feel jealous of attention a sibling is getting, jealous of someone's new sneakers, or jealous that a friend's parents let them go out on school nights when yours make you stay at home.

Occasional jealousy in a dating or crush situation is normal. Sometimes young people try to eliminate jealousy in a relationship by becoming more exclusive, for example, by dating only one person, promising to not text with another boy, etc. In fact, that kind of fix isn't a fix at all for jealousy because it only deals with the symptom of the problem and not the feeling of the insecurity that causes it.

In a healthy relationship—even in long-term, committed adult relationships—the two people involved know they cannot meet every emotional need their partner has. Each person will need to interact socially with people outside the relationship. What makes the partners feel secure in their love for each other is not the fact that they never text other people or never spend time with other people. The security comes from knowing they give something special to the partner that no one else can give.

You might be thinking something like "Um, if I am drenched in sweat and flustered every time my crush and I hold hands, how on earth would I have the confidence to feel I am that special to them?" As a young person just making your first steps into the dating world, it's hard to feel that degree of security in what you bring to a relationship. But the more you date and the more deep, mature friendships you develop, you will find yourself building confidence in your ability to make the people you care about feel cared about.

In the meantime, talking through jealous feelings, listening, and offering compromises are the best ways to deal with occasional relationship jealousy. For example, if you are feeling like your crush spends more time with their friends on weekends than with you, you can bring it up to them in a way that helps them understand what the emotional cost is for you. You could say, "It hurts my feelings when I don't see you all weekend but I know you're hanging out with your friends because I see the photos you post. It makes me feel like I'm only your girlfriend during the week, but that your weekend hours are too precious for me." Hopefully then your crush can explain how they see the situation and you can figure out a compromise together (maybe you see your crush every Saturday night, but weekend days are for their friends) that makes most sense for you.

Not Everyone Gets a Vote: Dealing with Third Party Interference

Another common problem in first dating relationships is a type of fishbowl effect. Because tweens and teens often have their first relationships in school, everything that happens between two people happens in front of everyone else. This means everyone knows all

The Trauma Text: When Your Friends Weigh In

Morgan, Brittany, Anna

What's up?

Morgan
Hey, why do you keep dating Jordan? He's such a dork.

Brittany
Yeah, I know he's nice but he dresses so weird.

Anna
It's really weird.

I like Jordan. He is very nice to me and makes me feel special. I don't care if he wears a scuba suit to algebra.

Morgan
But he's weird.

I like weird. I know you're trying to help, but everybody doesn't get a vote.

TIP

You might need to repeat this last line multiple times.

your business. This can make it hard to make your own decisions about what works and doesn't work for you in a relationship.

Social media has made this even harder. Now, if you change your status to be "social media official," not only does everyone know but also they can literally make comments about it!

It's not usually healthy for relationships, especially dating ones, to be completely secret. It's important that the adults who care about you know who you're hanging out with. It's also important that your close friends are able to talk with you about what they like and don't like when you are dating someone. This is an important safety concern and also it's fun (sometimes) to talk about your dates and crushes.

But not everyone in your world or in your social media world should get a vote on who you are dating and how you have a relationship. It's okay to tell people—online and in person—that you aren't actually looking for more people to share their opinion.

Age Differences in Relationships

When the adults in your life hear you want to date someone or have a crush, one of their first questions will probably be "how old are they?!" It can be especially tempting for girls to date older boys because in the early teen years, girls are further ahead in puberty than boys. A small age difference may not seem like a big deal, but dating someone your own age (or even better, in your own grade) means you'll have more in common and will always be safer.

When there is substantial age difference between two young people who are going out, the older partner is usually more experienced in dating and has fewer rules in place about when and who they can date. The older person might also have more access

to money because they have had summer jobs or a part-time job during the school year. All this means the older person usually has more power than the younger person. It's hard to make good decisions about what works in a relationship when there is this much of a power imbalance.

Fighting Fair: Boundaries and Consent

Just like jealousy, conflict is a normal part of every relationship. Don't you have minor fights with friends once in awhile? Disagreements with siblings? And your parents?

There are healthy ways to deal with conflict and there are ways that don't work as well. Try these on for starters:

❖ Find the best time to talk about things that are bugging you. If your crush is really worried about a math test, it's probably best to wait until you're in the same room and less stressed.

❖ Yes. In the same room. It is so tempting to have arguments via text, especially if you're mad and just want to get it out. But if you want to find a solution to the problem and not just have a fight (these are two very different things), wait until you can see each other, can hear tone of voice, see body language, etc. Don't be afraid to ask directly: "It seems like we're both getting upset. Can we wait and talk about this in person?" or "Can this be a phone call at least? I am worried we're going to just misunderstand each other in text."

❖ Make sure you're both in the room physically and in the room mentally. If you sit up in a chair and look at your crush instead of your phone (and they do the same), you increase the chance of understanding.

❖ Talk about your own feelings using "I" statements. For example, if you are frustrated because your date does not text you back quickly when you are trying to make plans, and you start with "You always take forever to get back to me about making plans," your partner is going to feel defensive and might stop listening. Instead, you could try something like "When we stop texting in the middle of a conversation when we're making plans, I feel confused and frustrated because I don't know how to schedule."

❖ On a related note, avoid words like "always" and "never," which are usually not accurate and also can feel like an attack.

❖ Speak up when you're upset about something, even if you can't do it that very minute. If you let things build up, it will be harder to have a discussion that leads to a positive end.

Breaking Up Is Hard to Do (Sometimes!)

When a relationship has too much conflict, doesn't feel equally good for both people, or doesn't have enough positive parts to make the effort worth it, you might start to think about breaking up. It's not always easy to know when it's time to break off a relationship, especially if you and your crush still enjoy spending time with one another.

It's especially difficult to figure out what to do when your relationship is very up and down—really good one minute and then bad the next. Relationships like this can be very exciting, and the roller coaster feelings might really liven up an otherwise boring semester of 8th grade. But even though roller coasters are exciting, you wouldn't want to ride one all day, would you? The same thing is true with roller coaster relationships: they can get very overwhelming and exhausting after a while.

If you decide that it's best for you and your crush to go separate ways, have a real talk about that decision. Have that real

talk in person, not via text message. Ghosting them (just disappearing over time) might seem nicer, but it's not; it's actually cruel. You can state your reasons in a general way ("We seem to have different values around how we spend our time" or "I was hoping to date someone who shared more of my interests"). You don't have to list everything they've ever done wrong since you started seeing them, but be clear that you don't want to continue the relationship.

Once you've broken up, you will have to figure out for yourself what will help you recover and feel better. You can start by spending more time with your friends and involving yourself in other activities. It's also important to give yourself some space to be sad, even if it was your idea to end your relationship. Find someone to talk with, journal about your feelings, or hang out with friends who care about you. It's also better for your emotional health if you don't get into another relationship the moment the first one ends. **Dealing with your feelings takes time.**

Stand Up for Yourself!

Up until now, we've been talking about normal conflict in a dating situation. In normal conflict, partners may fight, even be mad, but there is a bottom line no one crosses.

However, in some relationships, one partner crosses another's boundaries and becomes abusive. Abuse can take many different forms: verbal, emotional, or physical. Sometimes it's hard to tell if a relationship is actually abusive because your crush may also at times be very caring and attentive.

Warning signs that your relationship is no longer emotionally or physically safe for you might include if your partner:

❖ Doesn't respect your boundaries. For example, you might say you don't want them looking at your texts, but when you're not in the room, they pick up your phone and look anyway.

❖ Ignores your physical boundaries, especially when you say "no" or signal that you're uncomfortable.

❖ Insists that you should "check in" and gets upset if they don't know where you are all the time.

❖ Threatens you or says things that make you feel scared.

❖ Is constantly jealous and accuses you of cheating.

❖ Calls you names, even if they say they're "just joking."

❖ Pinches, scratches, or hits you, or breaks things that belong to you.

❖ Insists that you spend all your time with them and give up your own friends and activities.

If you feel like you might be in an abusive relationship, talk with a trusted adult right away so that you can figure out the best way to get out of the situation. And if you think you might be doing things that are actually abusive to your partner, you should also talk to a trusted adult. You can help with dealing with your feelings now, and make better choices, but it's important to do it when you are young and before this becomes a pattern.

Know the Facts:

A recent survey of tweens and teens revealed some very scary statistics about abuse in dating relationships:

* Many teens and tweens experience behavior that is abusive in dating relationships.

* The problem gets worse as teens get older, and abuse that starts in adolescent years can make adults more vulnerable to abuse later.

* 50% of teens who have been in a serious relationship say they've done something that went against their beliefs to please a partner.

* 20% of teens who have been in a serious relationship say that they have been slapped, hit, or pushed by a partner.

* Even though dating abuse is common, most tweens do not know what the early signs of abuse are or how to tell abuse from normal conflict.

Data from LoveIsRespect.org

Stand Up to Peer Pressure

In any relationship—whether a crush or a friendship—no one should be pushing you to do anything that makes you uncomfortable. When it comes to your crush, you deserve to be with someone who respects you and your boundaries. Part of puberty is the awakening of feelings of physical attraction, and these feelings can be mighty powerful. One of the easiest and most effective ways to slow down any physical interactions is by reinvesting in other kinds of fun together. Make a date to go to your

SLOW DOWN MISTER!

little brother's play, try a craft activity, experiment with a variety of cuisine you've never had, or play a new sport. And of course, don't forget the flip side: Never pressure someone to do anything that they don't want to do, either.

Stereotype Alert!
The Double Standards in Dating

Boys receive the message that they should be physical with girls. Girls, on the other hand, get the opposite message. You can see how these double standards can mix up the feelings of both young men and young women. It's understandable to be curious about physical involvement, but speak with a parent or a trusted adult about what is appropriate for you. The most important message about physical involvement is simply this: Trust your instincts. If something doesn't feel right, then it probably isn't. Always pull the reins and say "stop" if you feel uncomfortable for any reason, at any time!

Some Final Thoughts

For most girls, having crushes and learning to date is an important part of getting older, but it can be very challenging! And while no one said it's easy growing up, hopefully you got some tips from this book that will smooth the process along. Remember that making mistakes and occasionally getting rejected is all part of the process. It doesn't mean you are doing things wrong, just that you're building skills so you can have long, happy relationships of all kinds.

Not all relationships are easy, and sometimes things like jealousy and miscommunication can make them harder. Boundaries and jealousy can go hand-in-hand, as they do in this conversation.

What boundaries would you recommend for this couple to help Charlie manage his jealousy?

Charlie

I have been blowing up ur phone! Where R U?

I was at practice.

U should leave ur phone on anyway. What if I needed u for something?

What kind of something? Like a math emergency?

Not funny. I don't like it when I can't reach u.

Not always ur business!

I just wanna know where u r all the time. U make me worry.

I can't text you when I'm running around the soccer field. U want me to get kicked off the team?

Charlie (cont.)

If it comes between us then YES.

Don't play like that.

But I need 2 be able to reach u when I need to. How do I know u aren't with another dude?

It's an all girls team?!

TIP
from a
BESTIE

WHEN TO PUT
DOWN THE PHONE

"

My best friend and I used to play soccer in my backyard together after school, but the second she got her first iPhone in sixth grade, our whole friendship changed. All she wanted to talk about was boys, and she was texting guys from school constantly, even when we were hanging out. It hurt my feelings because I felt like she was ignoring me and always way more focused on her phone. And I stopped telling her really important stuff, because I didn't want to just text her about it. It made me miss her as a friend. So I decided to just tell her how I felt, and it was totally chill— she put away her phone for the first time in forever. Now we make sure that anything top secret is only shared IRL (in real life). Some stuff is just too important to blast out in a quick text!"

—Zinnia, age 14

About Applesauce Press Book Publishers

Good ideas ripen with time. From seed to harvest, Applesauce Press creates books with beautiful designs, creative formats, and kid-friendly information. Like our parent company, Cider Mill Press Book Publishers, our press bears fruit twice a year, publishing a new crop of titles each spring and fall.

"Where Good Books Are Ready for Press"

Visit us on the web at
www.cidermillpress.com
or write to us at
12 Spring St., PO Box 454
Kennebunkport, Maine 04046